How to Think Positive and be in Harmony with the World

15 Easy Steps

Your Gift

I wanted to show my appreciation that you support my work so I've put together a free gift for you.

http://bonusfreebook.org/

Just visit the link above to download it now.

I know you will love this gift.

If you like this book, you can see and buy my other books on this link:

ALL BOOKS OLIVER SMITH HERE

Thank you for attention!

With love,

OLIVER SMITH

Table of contents

INTRODUCTION

I want to thank you and congratulate you for downloading the book "Positive Thinking. A Simple Guide: How to Think Positive and Live In Harmony with the World".

This book contains proven strategies that will motivate you to achieve personal growth and have a positive attitude towards life. You need to have your own special purpose to become meaningful. Everyone is special in their own way. No one is worthless. Welcome to the world of Inspirational Living.

By now, I'm sure you understand that all the things you intend to do half-heartedly or halfway, never really reach completion. This is also the result we get when we lack of enthusiasm in our activities. It is the joy of doing things and seeing them through to completion that gives true fulfillment and motivation to work even harder.

Focus and determination is something this book will focus on. This is because you have to have an emphasis on what you want in life. It is vital if you want to achieve certain goals. Being determined is essential since it allows you to focus on your path. You will not have to rely on external forces and other people's success to find your motivation. Knowing what you want in life enables you to concentrates on your goals.

With this guide, you have an opportunity to start working on self-love, building positive thoughts, and deal with negative energy that usually deters your progress. You might not know this, but those people who you view as being better than you are never truly complete. Like you, they also lack certain things that they wish they had. In addition, the tendency to focus on materialistic goals always leads to misery. Instead of such goals, using happiness as a foundation to build better lives means that we struggle less; we also end up living with contentment.

Every chapter of this book covers very useful information. This information is meant to help you grow into a happier, better person. Enjoy!

Living in harmony with the World may prove to be difficult, especially, nowadays, when there are too many conflicts. In this chapter, we will discuss more on establishing and maintaining a healthy life/work balance by cultivating harmony. This is a reliable way to make progress in your personal and professional life.

1) Believe in yourself

Fear is a very common reason that normally stops people from achieving their goals. Do you actually believe in yourself? Lack of confidence should not be the reason for giving up. You need to be able to change this attitude and start believing that you have the power to conquer your fears. This is not to say that overcoming fear is easy, however, it is worth it!

In order to develop the confidence you need, you have to know where you want to be. This way you'll be able to explore your options. Set aside your feelings, thoughts and life experiences. Do not let these things become a stumbling block.

Another issue to contemplate concerns what you normally intend to do. For example, is the kind of person who normally puts other peoples' wishes before your own? People who tend to that are often overwhelmed with stress.

Believing in yourself means feeling good about yourself. It's about knowing your value and self-worth. But, most importantly it's all about finding your true identity.

2) Develop Inner harmony

a) Regular Meditation

A common misconception about meditation is that it has to be done in isolation. Meditation is all about relaxation and just letting your mind to wander freely. You might just set aside around 20 minutes every day to meditate. Do something relaxing like listen to soothing music or just sit quietly somewhere.

b) Praying

In a world where different groups of people have different religious inclinations, praying is vital in every sense. It ensures that you never stray spiritually; it also builds harmony inside us. Starting today, continuously try to start a dialogue with your Higher Power.

c) Thinking before reacting

Positive actions and reactions always play a huge role in establishing harmony. Our character will always determine who we are as individuals. Before you do something, consider whether your actions will matter afterward. There's no point in doing things that will have no impact tomorrow. Instead of helping you will just brew trouble. On the other hand, if you feel like your actions will be helpful in the future, deliberate on the best way to act or solve issues, and avoid doing things in a hurry or without thinking it through.

d) Clean up a Mess

Removing mess in your surroundings enables harmony to flow. This is one of the best ways to remove dissonance. Most people don't understand that junk brings about disharmony. Clean junk and eliminate mess in your environment.

e) Creating a harmonious environment

A harmonious environment will definitely make you become more peaceful. The results of staying in a harmonious environment are remarkable. You need to create an environment that cultivates your harmony. This may include, candlelit baths, reading before sleeping, taking walks in the park, etc.

f) Doing good deeds selflessly

In terms of being in harmony with people who live around you, the best way to achieve this is by doing good things to others without expecting anything in return. You will end up feeling better in your heart; you will also make new friends in the process.

g) Surround yourself with harmony

Apart from just creating an environment that is oozing with harmony, you also need to start surrounding yourself with harmonious people. This means looking for people who enjoy and cherish the value of peace. If you surround yourself with people who want to achieve harmony in their lives, then your goals will not be deterred. Think of this as the ideal support system to encourage you to grow daily in harmony.

h) Negativity of perfection

Perfection is one of the things that usually prevents growth and development of harmony. Only God is perfect, what we as humans can try to do is be our best. That we can achieve on a daily basis. We need to live our lives one day at a time, to make sure that we never regret our actions at the end of the day because we always think before we act!

3) Manage everyday stresses

Stress is something that all people experience on a daily basis. From not getting enough sleep to body pains, to worrying too much, the list of types of stresses is endless. But first, before we discuss more on how we can reduce stress in our lives, we have to understand what actually takes place in our bodies when we are under stress.

Changes that occur in our bodies when we are under stress include;

- Increased heart rate
- Increased blood pressure
- Increase metabolism
- Increase respiration

This reaction is meant to assist you to respond to high-pressure situations. If however, this reaction becomes a norm, your health becomes adversely affected and your general wellbeing is damaged.

How to Reduce or Control Stress

There are several ways to deal with stress. Some may prove to be more effective than other. Keep in mind that in order to fully control stress, you have to exercise patience. You have to be persistent and determined to overcome the stress itself. You may also be forced to make some small lifestyle changes as well. Reduce stress by:

- Exercise
- Take up hobbies
- Share your feelings
- Be flexible
- Avoid doing too many things at once
- Visualize
- Meditate

- Be realistic

Alternative Process of Controlling stress:

- Start by listing down the main causes of stress in your life.
- Note down how this stress affects your life (family, job, body etc.)
- Differentiate you stresses and groups them into short-term stresses and long-term stresses.
- Look for a suitable support system that will help you to make some positive changes (family, friends, and professional help).
- Note down the obstacles that may discourage you from ending the stress.
- Make note of lifestyles and behaviors that you can change or give up to reduce stress
- List down what changes worked and which ones didn't and use this information to make better changes.

4) Know easy ways to relax

Sometimes all you need is a quick relaxation fix when stressed out. Whether you are at home or at work these tips will help you to feel relaxed almost immediately.

- **Staring upwards and counting down from 60 to 0:** This tip helps relieve stress. It also lowers your blood pressure because you will start to breathe slowly as you countdown. This method is particularly effective for individuals whose minds are easily distracted.
- **Writing down your worries and setting it aside for tomorrow:** Suppose there's something disturbing you and you'd like to settle it. It would be helpful if you just wrote it down on a piece of paper. Your mind will be at ease since you know that the issue has been noted and that you will deal with it later. You'll be able to rest at that moment.
- **Using Imagery to meditate:** This is a very powerful technique of relaxing. This is because imagery gives you a brief escape from daily tensions and fears. Make sure that you use all your five senses to aid your peaceful imagination.
- **Breathing exercises:** A good way to lower your heart rate is through taking deep breaths. Not only will you be calm, you will also be able to concentrate on your body, and block outside obstruction. Focus on your stomach makes when you take deep breaths. Also, make sure that you breathe out from your mouth. Do this exercise for 10 minutes.

- **Muscle exercise:** Whenever you slowly tense and ease your muscles for some time, you can progressively reduce mental anxiety and your muscles will also feel more relaxed.

Ever hear the famous saying "Laughter is the Best Medicine"? And this doesn't refer to fake laughter where the back of your head hurts. True laughter is a very strong medicine. Humor stimulates healthy emotional and physical changes in our bodies. The many ways through which humor assists our bodies also includes:

- Diminishing pain
- Relaxes the whole body
- Protects the heart
- Humor triggers the release of endorphins
- Lowers stress hormones
- Improves your mood
- Boosts immune system
- Protects our bodies from the harmful effects of stress

Apart from that, humor also improves our relationships with others, it boosts our emotional health and we tend to live longer if we laugh.

Ever wonder what happened? As a child, you probably laughed all the time. But now that you're all grown up, you've become more serious. You laugh less and deny yourself medication that supposed to be natural.

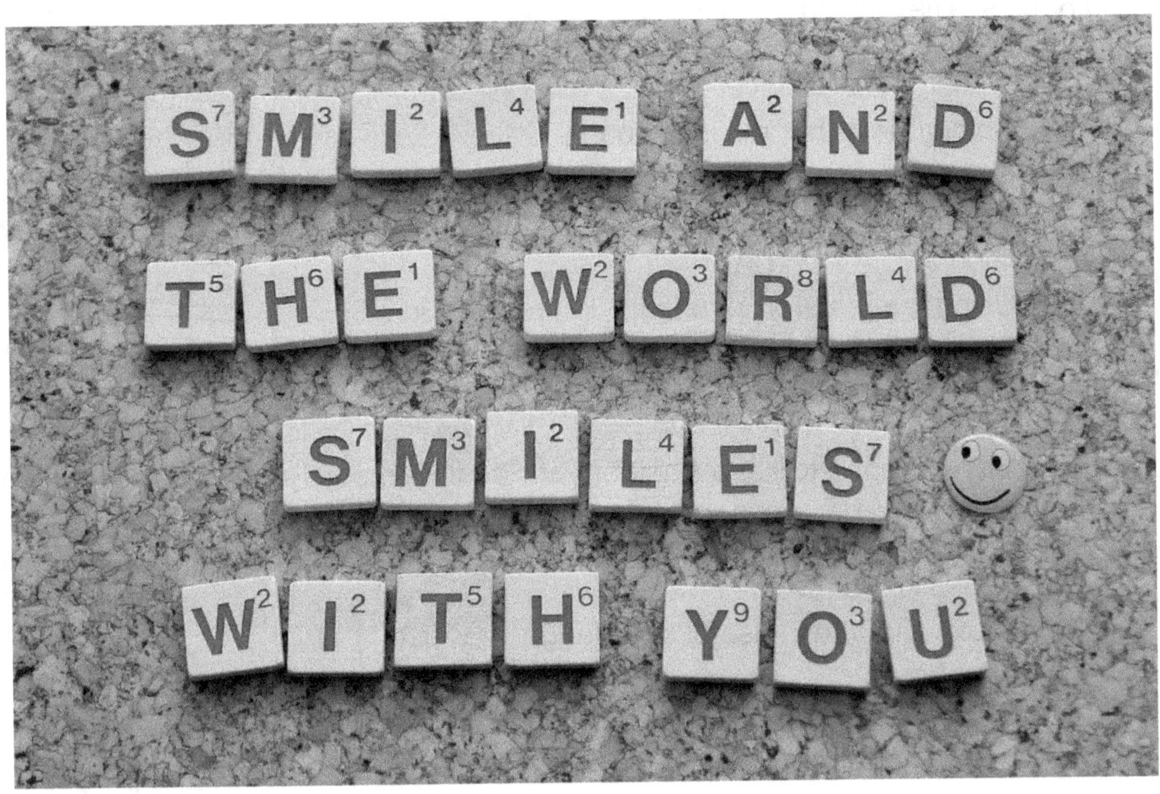

Simply put, self-motivation is a life skill, the force that motivates you to do things. You need the motivation to push you to achieve your goals, to feel more contented and improve your quality of life. Understanding and growing your self-motivation can assist you to dominate many aspects of your life.

Motivation is made up of four key elements:

- Optimism
- Initiative
- Commitment
- Personal Drive

We tend to live better lives when we love what we do. In fact, if we enjoy our work, then it can be a lot easier to deal with stresses those come with it.

<u>**Skills involved in Self-motivation**</u>

There are several skills that are involved in self-motivation. Did you know that motivated people are in a better position to motivate others? These skills are imperative in leadership roles. They include:

- Taking the right level of risk
- Setting great but realistic goals
- Being committed to personal and work goals
- Seeking opportunities actively and grasping them when the chance avails itself
- Using feedback to constantly improve yourself
- Dealing with setbacks and obstacles the right way
- Persistence in pursuing your goals

As the last point, you have to keep track of your achievements and ambitions while still staying motivated. In order to maintain high motivation levels you can try to do the following:

- Learn and obtain useful knowledge
- Stay Positive
- Keep enthusiastic people around you
- Have a "do-it" attitude
- Understand your weakness and strengths
- Help others and seek help yourself

1) Choosing your goals

You need to start setting the right goals and use those goals to determine your journey in this life. The truth is that setting the right goals will always bring success in your life. However, a point of concern is about being successful but missing out on the joys of life when by the time that you're already successful. You don't want to be the guy who works too hard just to make friends. Such situations arise if you do not set the right goals in your life. Luckily this book will help you set the right goals.

a) Never Set Goals for the Wrong Reasons

The right goals will definitely bring you an awesome life if you achieve them, however, the wrong goals will bring you the exact opposite. Most people like to set goals based on the destination i.e. "buying a car". What they tend to overlook is the journey to reaching that destination. Instead of setting goals based on the destination switch it around and set your goals based on the life journey that you would like to take.

b) Chose goals to create journeys

You need to choose a life direction that you want to take. Using this, you can then create an exciting, profound, fascinating journey. Know how you want to spend your life, the activities that you want to do on a daily basis, how you want to spend your extra time and who you want to team up with.

c) Change Goals that don't work

This is a good technique to use to have a meaningful journey, one that is almost entirely fun-filled! You have to understand that it's never too late to change your goals. You always have a chance to change your life in a way that satisfies you. Instead of setting goals just to change your life, change your life first be getting involved with the activities that you like to do and then chose goals that will guide you towards the life that you want.

2) What is your visualization

Before believing in your goals, it is necessary that you have an idea of what it looks like. This is the sole purpose of visualization. Using visualization one is able to create a mental image of what the future beholds. If you decide to visualize an outcome that you want, you will begin to see the likelihood of achieving that goal. By catching a glimpse of your preferred outcome, you become motivated. You start to prepare yourself to pursue that goal.

Visualization is not dreaming, or simply just hoping for a better future. It is a properly premeditated process of performance management and improvement that is supported by many successful people around the world.

Why it always Works

Visualization is effective because all neurons in the human brain which are responsible for transmitting information, interpret brain imagery as if it was a real-life manifestation. Whenever you visualize something the brain generates impulses that alert neurons to perform the act that you have envisioned. If this is done continuously, our body becomes primed to act the same way we visualize.

Anyone can benefit from the usefulness of visualization. It is an important aspect of success because it keeps you bound to your goals and ambitions. Ultimately, it increases your chances of achieving your goals.

Types of Visualization

- **Outcome Visualization:** This is where you visualize yourself achieving certain goals. You begin to create a profound mental image of an anticipated outcome using all your senses. After doing this, you then begin to harbor this image in your mind. For some people, they like to write down their imaginations so that they list all the details, the thrills, the satisfaction etc. This image is what will keep you motivated.
- **Process Visualization:** This different type of visualization involves envisaging each step involved to attain an outcome. In order to achieve your goal, one must strive to complete each step instead of just envisioning the desired outcome. You have to visualize yourself completing each step distinctly. You also have to use optimistic conceptual imagery to maintain your focus and motivation. This will help you to overcome hurdles and setbacks.

In all honesty, visualization can never replace hard work period. However, practice, combined with visualization can prove to be very effective. It is a very great technique to achieve positive outcomes. You will also notice a change in your behavior as well as your life.

If you come up with reasonable plans, you can make your dreams come true. This means finding ways to overcome any setbacks you come across the road. In order to get started, there are several stages that you'll need to:

a) Be specific with your dream

Specifying your dream will help you focus on making it happen. You can begin by writing down your dream in a notebook or just writing down an idea of what you want to achieve.

b) Turn your dream into a burning desire

This will ensure that you develop a strong will that'll come in handy when you get to go through challenging points of the process. The best way to ensure that you hoard this burning desire is by actually believing that you can really achieve your dreams.

c) Turn your desires into goals

In order to actually turn your burning desires into realistic goals, you have to first believe in your desires. This means that you need to be committed to working on your goals now.

d) Take Action

After setting realistic goals you will have to make a plan and start acting on it right away. Use every opportunity that comes your way to start getting things done. Avoid adjourning your actions because you'll start to complicate the process and you won't make any progress.

e) Set short-term goals

Since you already have your main goals set, you'll have to subdivide the goals into smaller objectives that are more workable.

f) Constantly check your progress

In order stay motivated you need to constantly check your progress. It doesn't really matter if your progress is not going through as fast as you'd wish it to. The most important thing is that you are moving forward.

g) Enjoy the journey

If you do not enjoy the whole process then the dream isn't worth following. Make sure that you enjoy the entire process for there to be meaning after you have achieved your dream.

4) Everyday exercises

In order to stay focus and motivated in life, you have to stay in shape. Fitness will help you to maintain your general health and mental balance. Start living a healthy lifestyle today by increasing your energy, and losing some body weight. Exercise will also reduce your risks of contracting diseases like diabetes, heart diseases, blood pressure etc. Physical practitioners recommended that people do aerobic exercises at least three times a week. This should be done for 20 minutes each session.

Several factors will determine whether the exercises you perform are effective or not; they include:

- Choice of exercise

- Intensity
- Frequency

There are several moderate intensity exercises you can decide to choose from. It will help if you enjoy doing it. They might seem simple but they have a significant impact on your body and general wellbeing.

Stretching

This is one of the most effective exercises you can start doing today. Stretching awakens your body as well as your mind. Let stretching be a part of your daily routine. Stretch your muscles, paying attention to all groups of body muscles. Starting each exercise by stretching is also a good way to reduce the risk of injury; it also improves your flexibility. The many benefits of stretching include:

- Improves flexibility and posture.
- Reduces muscle injury during workouts.
- Releases muscle tension.
- Enhances blood supply throughout the body.
- You'll feel calmer and you will also have a peaceful mindset.

Walking

Physicians say that walking for more than 30 minutes helps to be physically strong and agile. This is one of the simplest exercises you can do every day. Walking is effective, especially if you are getting older. By walking daily you can reduce the risk of ailments such as osteoporosis. Start walking regularly to improve your sense of purpose and self-worth. Other benefits of walking include:

- Reduces risk of premature death.
- Reduces your chances of getting diabetes, high blood pressure, colon cancer and hypertension.
- Aids in weight loss.
- Improves sense of balance, strength, and flexibility.

Dancing

Dancing is particularly effective if you want to relieve yourself of stress. Your bones also become stronger when you dance. Make sure that you dance at least twice a week to stay youthful and maintain your agility. You always express a lot of stuff whenever you are dancing i.e. your emotions, opinions, and feelings. It is very refreshing to dance alone when no one else is around. Dancing is the cheapest form of entertainment you can have. Given the many variations of dances in the world, just chose one that makes you comfortable and happy.

Jogging

Jogging is so beneficial and it is also not stressful as pace-running. It is a very popular exercise that ensures you stay healthy. It is also an inexpensive exercise when compared to the yoga and dancing. Jogging has the ability to prolong a person's life expectancy. Ensure that you don't overdo it. You want to do exercises that leave you refreshed and not fatigued or with muscle stress. Start a regular jogging routine to improve your blood pressure, mental health, bone health, HDL cholesterol etc.

5) The leader in life

Leaders are normally highly self-motivated people. They are set apart from the rest because of their actions, behavior, and the way they think. You have to take up a leadership role to improve your chances of becoming a more productive person. This means becoming more responsible, focused, determined, motivated and being able to endure hardships.

These are the traits that you should develop to become an effective leader. You also have to be good at making decisions in order to manage your time productively. Being a leader means you have to change certain aspects of your lifestyle and embrace a lifestyle that will positively influence on people are around you.

Motivation needs to play a huge role in defining who you are as a leader; a leader who stands out from the rest. Through motivation, you will have the courage to develop new skills that will surely make a difference. You'll feel obliged to alter the situations of the people who look up to you. You will start to become more responsible.

Leadership is not a hereditary trait like most people believe; anyone can become a leader if they wanted to. There's also some degree of pressure that comes with leadership. This pressure is meant to help you to adopt in order to grow and shape you into a progressive person. You will be able to maximize your efficiency to achieve your goals as well as those of your people. A successful leader always lives a life that is full of satisfaction.

Starting today you need to embrace all opportunities that come your way. Using your leadership skills take on small tasks as you advance to more advanced challenges. With time you will realize how influential leadership can be in terms of enhancing your wellbeing. You have an opportunity to view the world from a different perspective.

1) The power of thanksgiving

The simple meaning of "Thanksgiving" is about simply expressing gratitude, to be grateful for the life that we have. If truth be told, this is one of the most vital traits that we need to perfect. Gratitude is never limited, it's always the best thing you can do during good times, and it is also the one thing that you should do during bad times. It draws our hearts to appreciate being alive and we begin to consider the lives of others.

The power of thanksgiving takes into account of the following facts:

- That being grateful normally unlocks many opportunities
- That blessing follows us when we are appreciative other people's deeds
- That faith strengthens our motives

- Those blessings in our lives always repel corrupt energy
- That gratitude motives us to always move forward to world of new opportunities
- That we are who we are because of the one who created us
- That gratitude is a service meant for all

Thanksgiving is fundamental to anyone who wants to progress in life.

2) My spiritual life

Do you know that the objective of any spiritual life is to surrender to a higher power? To be offered freedom and infinite possibilities by that higher power. To surrender means that you believe and trust that a higher power has the ability to accomplish anything even if you cannot predict an outcome.

With the right level of spirit, most events habitually unfold seamlessly. You never have to struggle with much; you also never have to use a lot of force to accomplish your tasks. A person who is controlled by their ego is someone who is 'lonely'. They are constantly trying to survive this 'inimical' world.

You have to free your conscious of fears or any doubt about your future. Never let your ego control who you really are. Use the following tips to help you with your spiritual life

- Find your intentions
- Set your intents high
- Know that a higher power looks over you every day
- Discern that everyone else is also in the realm of the higher power
- Reinforce your plans every day you wake up
- Forgive others and forgive yourself
- Learn to let go when wronged
- Revere the holy life
- Embrace new things and possibilities

3) The key to success and happiness

Success is more gratifying if you are also happy. However, people have different implications on how they view these two things. The reason most people are still not happy or successful is that they spend most of their time harboring negative emotions and thoughts.

In order to advance in life, you need to stop spending much of your time being unhappy and feeling unsuccessful. This can be done only if you are willing enough to work towards attaining the right key or keys for that matter. There are six keys which are essential to getting the life everyone desires. They include:

- Being present
- Gratitude
- Proper time management
- Setting smart, achievable goals
- Empowering morning routines
- Prioritizing health and well being

4) Creating a positive atmosphere

Being moody all the time can sometimes become contagious. To create a positive atmosphere you must embrace a positive feeling and bear that feeling all the way through. The suggestions below will help you to improve your attitude and model your behavior towards a positive ambiance. Try these five tips to create a more positive

- Spread Happiness
- Celebrate wins
- Change your response tactics
- Have fun
- Be kind to people

Positive habits build positive lives when practiced often. It is a good thing to maintain positive habits because you end up growing to be a better person. Therefore you need to start mastering several positive habits from today. This will be determined by the choices you decide to make on a daily basis. These choices will determine your actions, thoughts, and they will ultimately influence on your life. Actions and thoughts are the building blocks of the habits that define our lives. If we give up our bad habits, we have an opportunity to embrace new ones that are more positive. In this section, we will discuss ten positives that can help anyone to improve their life.

1. **Positive thinking:** Positive thinkers always have a huge impact on our societies. You have to understand that positive thoughts have the ability to reduce your stress levels. Let positive thoughts improve your health and

general well-being. Life will certainly be more interesting if you become more positive about life itself. Never let negativity to lead you astray.

2. **Healthy Eating:** Stay healthy by eating food that is rich in vital nutrients that your body requires; avoid eating junk if you can, but if you must, exercise to reduce the negative effects it has. Good food will always make you smarter and healthier. You will be fit enough to pursue all your goals.

3. **Hard work:** This is a fact of life, that for anyone to be successful, he or she has to be a hardworking person. Idleness will never go hand in hand with hope, especially if you want to be financially successful and happy. You need to understand that without hard work, it is almost impossible to realize your life goals and dreams.

4. **Listening more:** Communication is essential if you want to have any kind of relationship. It is also the best way through which you can learn more than you already know. A good listener relates better to others and is also more productive.

5. **Reading:** You need to start embracing the culture or reading new materials. People who read regularly tend to display better reasoning skills. They are also very confident.

6. **Goal setting:** You cannot set out on a journey without knowing your destination. Develop a habit of setting achievable goals to prepare for a better future. Let motivation turn your ambitions into a reality.

7. **Waking up early:** This is a common habit of most successful people. They understand that waking up early make them wiser and healthier. Apart from these positive effects, you will be more productive if you wake up early.

8. **Mindfulness:** Be mindful of other people, their work, their emotions, and their opinions. Cultivate mindfulness in your thought process to improve your awareness of the occurrences in your life. This will enable other people to understand and accommodate you even though you might have different views about life in general.

9. **Show Gratitude:** Being grateful goes a long way, especially if you believe in the Law of attraction i.e. good deeds attract more good deeds. In the spirit of positivity, strive to make the best out of life. Never sit around to regret or complain about the past.

10. **Exercising:** As discussed earlier, exercising is one trait that should be viewed as mandatory. Generate the energy your body requires for day-to-day activities through exercises. You will definitely appreciate the difference.

CONCLUSION

It is my hope that this book helped you understand what is required of you to build a better life and most importantly manifest success in all areas. Every effort you make including reading the book won't go unrewarded because the knowledge gained will not only change your life but also people around you. It is, therefore, your responsibility to put into practice all that you have learned for you to learn that all efforts put into having this book was it all worth it.

Your Gift

I wanted to show my appreciation that you support my work so I've put together a free gift for you.

http://bonusfreebook.org/

Just visit the link above to download it now.

I know you will love this gift.

If you like this book, you can see and buy my other books on this link:

ALL BOOKS OLIVER SMITH HERE

Thank you for attention!

With love,

OLIVER SMITH

BONUS

To our customers we give a discount to $10,

it's very easy to get it, use the coupon code

on the link

HERE